Liquids

William B. Rice

Consultant

Scot Oschman, Ph.D.
Palos Verdes Peninsula Unified School District
Rancho Palos Verdes, California

Publishing Credits

Dona Herweck Rice, *Editor-in-Chief*; Lee Aucoin, *Creative Director*; Don Tran, *Print Production Manager;* Timothy J. Bradley, *Illustration Manager*; Chris McIntyre, *Editorial Director*; James Anderson, *Associate Editor*; Jamey Acosta, *Associate Editor*; Jane Gould, *Editor*; Peter Balaskas, *Editorial Administrator*; Neri Garcia, *Senior Designer*; Stephanie Reid, *Photo Editor*; Rachelle Cracchiolo, M.S.Ed., *Publisher*

Image Credits

cover pulsar75/Shutterstock; p.1 pulsar75/Shutterstock; p.4 Charlie Hutton/Shutterstock; p.5 Elena Yakusheva/Shutterstock; p.6 (left) Lane V. Erickson/Shutterstock, (center) Elena Yakusheva/Shutterstock, (right) Lisa H/Shutterstock; p.7 Sebastian Duda/Shutterstock; p.8 Zaneta Baranowksa/Shutterstock; p.9 (left) Valentyn Volkov/Shutterstock, (right) Eric Isselee/Shutterstock; p.10 Tim Bradley, p.11 (left) Darren Hedges/Shutterstock, (right) Tischenko/Shutterstock; p.12 TranceDrumer/Shutterstock; p.13 Can Balcioglu/Shutterstock; p.14 juliengrondin/Shutterstock; p.15 Johnny Lye/Shutterstock; p.16 Jupiterimages; p.17 Jupiterimages; p.18 Epic Stock/Shutterstock; p.19 cbpixa/Shutterstock; p.20 Lev Kropotov/Shutterstock; p.21 Can Balcioglu/Shutterstock;p.22 Romeo Koitmae/Shutterstock; p.23 Hemera Technologies; p.24-25 (from L to R) Lev Kropotov/Shutterstock, Julien Grondin/Shutterstock, Olga Lyubkina/Shutterstock, Olga Lyubkina/Shutterstock, Julian Rovagnati/Shutterstock; p.26 Andrey Armyagov; p.27 (background) silver-john/Shutterstock, (foreground) Cheryl Casey/Shutterstock; p.28 Rocket400 Studio/Shutterstock; p.29 Ana Clark; p.32 Martha Davis

Teacher Created Materials
5301 Oceanus Drive
Huntington Beach, CA 92649-1030
http://www.tcmpub.com

ISBN 978-1-4333-1414-8

Table of Contents

A World of Matter

Look around you. Smell the air. Touch a chair. Did you know that everything you see, smell, and touch is **matter**? Matter is the stuff that makes up everything. *Everything*. This book is matter. You are matter, too. Every inch of you!

Everything you see here is made of matter.

Everything you see here is made of matter, too.

States of Matter

But not all matter is the same. Matter comes in different forms called **states of matter**. One state is solid. This book is solid. Rocks, ice cubes, and your feet are solids, too!

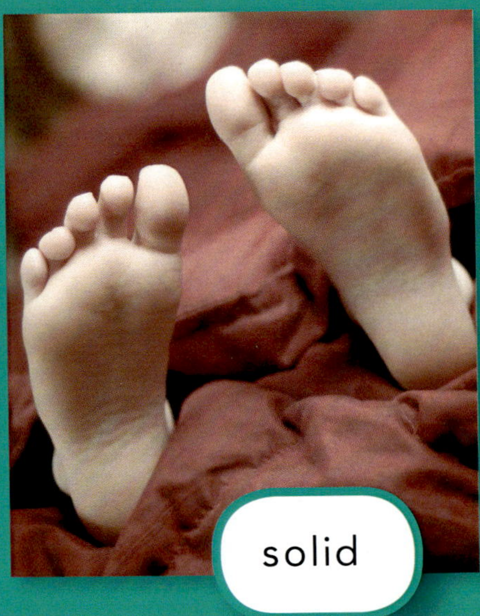

One state is gas. The air around you is gas. Steam from a hot bowl of soup is also a gas.

A third state of matter is liquid. What is a liquid?

Melted Ice

Watch an ice cube melt. What you see tells you something about liquids.

A liquid is a state of matter that is **fluid**. To be fluid means to flow, like water or melted ice cream. A liquid has no set shape. Its shape changes all the time.

A liquid's shape is easily changed.

But a liquid does have a set **volume**. The volume is the amount of space a liquid takes up.

Fun Fact

If you take water from a cup and put it in a bowl, the shape of the water changes. But it is still the same amount of water.

The state of matter depends on different things. One thing is the space between its **particles** (PAR-ti-kuhls). Particles are the tiny parts that make up matter.

A solid has *less* space between particles than a liquid does. A gas has *more* space between particles than a liquid does.

When matter is a solid, the particles are close together. When matter is a liquid, the particles have more space between them. When matter is a gas, the particles are really far apart.

Fun Fact

When a candle burns, it changes from a solid to a liquid to a gas. Think about it!

Matter can change. Heat is one thing that changes matter. Particles start to move apart when matter is heated. A solid can begin to melt. It becomes a liquid. When the liquid is heated, it becomes a gas.

Fun Fact

When liquid becomes a gas, that is called evaporation (i-vap-uh-REY-shun).

This steam is evaporation from the hot liquid in the kettle.

When gas cools, it becomes liquid again. This is called **condensation** (kon-den-SEY-shun). You see condensation every time you have a cold drink.

Fun Fact

Can rock become a liquid? Yes! Lava is really hot rock.

Warm air outside the cold glass cools down. The air cools and becomes a liquid. You see the liquid on the outside of the glass. The glass is not leaking. It is just condensation!

All About Liquids

You may already know when something is a liquid. But how do you know? You know by its **properties**. Properties are how something looks, feels, or acts. The properties of a liquid are what make it a liquid.

For example, can a liquid change shape? Yes, it has the property of changing shape. A liquid takes the shape of whatever holds it. It changes shape if it is placed in something else. It also changes shape if it is moved.

Water in the ocean changes shape as the Earth moves and the wind blows.

Another property of liquids is the volume. Can the volume of a liquid be changed?

Imagine a bowl filled with water. Now imagine that you pour the water into a smaller bowl and try to squish all the water inside. Can you do it? No, the water does not squish down. It comes out instead. That is because you cannot change the volume of a liquid.

Fun Fact

When water gets hot enough, it becomes a gas.

Another property of a liquid is that it can flow. That means it can move along. Think of melting ice cream or water in a stream. Both of those liquids flow. Every liquid does.

As the ice cream becomes a liquid, it flows down the girl's arm!

One more property of liquid is the way its particles behave. The particles of a liquid are close but not tight. They move around each other.

Each of these has all the properties of a liquid.

The particles change place all the time. That is why liquids can change shape and flow. Their particles let them do it.

A Wet World

The world seems like a pretty solid place. But look again! From great big oceans to tiny drops of sweat, it's a wet, wet, wet world of liquids!

Science Lab: What Is Condensation?

See condensation in action by doing this lab.

Materials:

- 3 glasses, all the same size
- freezer
- cold colored liquid such as fruit punch

Procedure:

1. Look at the glasses. See how they are all the same.
2. Put two glasses on a table, away from each other.
3. Leave the first glass empty. Pour cold colored liquid in the second glass.
4. Put the third glass in the freezer.

5 Leave the glasses for 15 minutes.

6 Take the glass out of the freezer and put it on the table away from the others.

7 Look at the glasses. Which ones have condensation and why? The empty glass that stayed on the table has no condensation. The two other glasses have condensation. They got colder than the air around them. The warmer air touched the cold glasses. That turned the air into a liquid.

Glossary

condensation—the act of changing a gas to a liquid

evaporation—the act of changing a liquid to a gas

fluid—flowing, or something that flows

matter—anything that takes up space

particles—the tiny parts of something

properties—the ways that an object looks, feels, and acts

states of matter—the different forms that matter can take, including solid, liquid, and gas

volume—amount of space something takes up

Index

A Scientist Today

Martha Davis is a leader. She works with other scientists to protect the most important liquid on Earth: water. Her work has helped to bring back Mono Lake in California! The lake was dying, but it is thriving again thanks to Martha and others like her.